THE STORY BEHIND

PAPER

Barbara A. Somervill

Heinemann Library
Chicago, Illinois

www.heinemannraintree.com
Visit our website to find out more information about Heinemann-Raintree books.

To order:
☎ Phone 888-454-2279
🖥 Visit www.heinemannraintree.com to browse our catalog and order online.

Edited by Megan Cotugno and Diyan Leake
Designed by Philippa Jenkins
Original illustrations © Capstone Global Library Ltd.
Illustrated by Oxford Designers and Illustrators
Picture research by Hannah Taylor and Mica Brancic
Production by Eirian Griffiths
Originated by Capstone Global Library
Printed in China by CTPS

15 14 13 12 11
10 9 8 7 6 5 4 3 2 1

Library of Congress Cataloging-in-Publication Data
Somervill, Barbara A.
 The story behind paper / Barbara A. Somervill.
  p. cm.—(True stories)
 Includes bibliographical references and index.
 ISBN 978-1-4329-5438-3 (hc)
 1. Paper. I. Title.
 TS1105.S676 2012
 676—dc22
                                    2010042103

Acknowledgments
The author and publishers are grateful to the following for permission to reproduce copyright material: akg-images p. 6; Alamy pp. 10 (© Interfoto), 16 (© Photobywayne), 19 (© Danita Delimont), 22 (© brt COMM); Alamy Image p. 21 bottom (© The Art Gallery Collection); Corbis p. 9 (© Bettmann); Getty Images p. 8 (Hulton Archive); istockphoto p. 15 (© Paul Rodriguez); Photolibrary p. 23 (White/Harnett/Hanzon Harnett/ Hanzon); Science Photo Library p. 13 (Power and Syred); Shutterstock pp. 4 (© S1001), 5 (© Y-tea), 12 (© Eric Milos), 17 (© Alaettin Yildirim), 18 (© Dmitry Kalinovsky), 20 (© fotohunter), 24 (© Huguette Roe), 27 (© Anthony Hall), 21 top (© Andrew Olscher), iii (© Discpicture), 11 (© Moreno Soppelsa), 26 (© design56); The Art Archive p. 7.

Cover photograph of stack of crumpled papers reproduced with permission of Getty Images (Stone+/Paul Taylor).

We would like to thank Ann Fullick for her invaluable help in the preparation of this book.

Every effort has been made to contact copyright holders of any material reproduced in this book. Any omissions will be rectified in subsequent printings if notice is given to the publisher.

Disclaimer
All the Internet addresses (URLs) given in this book were valid at the time of going to press. However, due to the dynamic nature of the Internet, some addresses may have changed, or sites may have changed or ceased to exist since publication. While the author and publisher regret any inconvenience this may cause readers, no responsibility for any such changes can be accepted by either the author or the publisher.

Contents

Some words are shown in bold, **like this**. You can find out what they mean by looking in the glossary.

Paper All Around Us

▲ The day's news is printed on a type of paper called **newsprint.**

We have paper all around us. Much of the food we eat is packaged in paper. We use wallpaper to cover our walls. We read newspapers, books, and magazines printed on paper, and we wipe up messes with paper towels. Students do homework in paper notebooks.

For fun, we read graphic novels, fly paper kites, and do arts and crafts projects with colored construction paper. We decorate bedroom walls with posters, and we record memories in scrapbooks. When the mail comes, paper arrives in the form of bills, letters, advertisements, and birthday cards.

Most of this paper is made from wood **pulp**, which is produced by grinding up trees. Paper can also be made from cotton, linen, silk, or even rice and bamboo. Some paper is made from synthetic (human-made) materials, such as latex or plastic.

Uses for paper

Throughout the world, paper is used in hundreds of different ways. Canadian builders lay waterproof paper under roof shingles. Germans sell juice in waxed paper containers. The Chinese use rice paper for the beautiful art of writing called calligraphy—and for spring rolls, which are vegetables and pork or shrimp wrapped in rice paper and deep-fried. (Yes, people eat the paper!) The Japanese use a special paper, called *shoji gami*, to make sliding doors that separate rooms.

Paper money

Throughout the world, paper money is made with cloth **fibers** (pieces), which are strong and can take a lot of use. A $10 bill and a British £5 note each last about three years before wearing out.

▼ **Brilliant red Chinese paper lanterns light up the night.**

The History of Paper

▲ Ancient papers were mostly made with rags.

The word "paper" comes from "papyrus," a kind of plant. The ancient Egyptians pounded papyrus into sheets and used it as a writing surface about 5,000 years ago. Papyrus was more like thin sheets of wood than paper, however.

Ancient China

The first people to make paper similar to the paper we use today were the Chinese. Evidence shows that the Chinese wrote on paper made from the fabric linen as early as 8 BCE.

During the Han dynasty (202 BCE–220 CE), Chinese paper was made from a mix of materials, including rags. In 105 CE, a Chinese clerk named Ts'ai Lun pounded rags, fishnets, and the bark of a mulberry tree into pulp and pressed the pulp flat. When it dried, Ts'ai had writing paper.

Early Chinese paper was thicker and tougher than paper today. The heavy fibers made excellent clothing and, when several sheets were used together, it could even be used as armor in battle. The Chinese did not use paper as their main material for writing until about 200 CE.

Trading paper

Paper, like silk and spices, was soon traded to other parts of the world. By 610 papermaking had spread north to Korea and Japan, and westward to India and Arab cultures. By the 700s, people in Baghdad, in present-day Iraq, had learned how to make paper. From Baghdad, papermaking reached Morocco, in North Africa, about 200 years later. Moroccan papermakers used **flax** and other plant fibers for pulp.

The first paper money

Chinese began using paper money about 960 BCE. Paper money replaced the need to carry heavy purses filled with coins.

◀ **Chinese people during the Sung dynasty (960 BCE–279 CE) used paper money like this.**

▲ Early papermaking was done by hand.

Paper in Europe

When paper finally reached Europe, around the 1000s, few people were interested in it. At that time, the Roman Catholic Church was very powerful. The Church thought paper was an Arab invention and did not want Catholics to use paper. Instead, the Church insisted on using **parchment** and **vellum**, which were both made from animal skins. In 1221 Holy Roman Emperor Frederick II said official documents written on paper were illegal. But paper was cheaper than parchment, and slowly people became interested in cheaper writing materials.

Italy

By 1100 Italy had become the papermaking center of Europe. Italian papermakers developed pulp **mills**, which were large buildings dedicated to papermaking. Machines called **presses** helped to dry paper into flat sheets. The Italians also introduced wire screen **molds** and presses. Finished paper was dried on ropes, like sheets on a clothesline.

Increased demand

In the 1200s and 1300s, books were very expensive. Each book had to be copied by hand, and Catholic religious men called **monks** handwrote most books over many months. In 1439 German inventor Johannes Gutenberg developed a **movable-type printing press**. Gutenberg's press made printing books faster. As the number of books printed increased, the demand for paper increased.

Papermakers continued to develop new, better, more efficient mill machinery. Europeans made beaters (much like today's food processors) to turn rags into pulp faster. They made finer molds and better presses that used new kinds of machinery. Writing paper, newspapers, books, and magazines became part of the ever-growing demand for paper.

▼ Printing books increased the demand for paper.

▲ Papermaking was hard work in the 19th century.

Papermaking by machines

Beginning in the 1700s, the Industrial Revolution began. This was a time when power-driven machines replaced making products by hand. This brought many more changes to the paper **industry**. In 1798 British papermaker J. N. L. Robert developed the first flat-screen papermaking machine, which was a device that spread pulp smoothly on a flat screen.

A few years later, French chemist Claude-Louis Berthollet discovered a way to bleach pulp and produce very white paper. Before Bertholett, paper was a pale brownish color, which made it more difficult to read the print.

At this time, rags were still often used to make paper. But in 1843 German inventor Friedrich Keller developed a machine that ground wood into pulp. From then on, wood-pulp paper replaced rag-made paper. Paper, once produced sheet by sheet, became larger, stronger, softer, and thinner. Papermaking changed from a skilled craft to an industry with factories.

Making paper in modern times

As mills expanded, paper companies bought forestland and began logging and **processing** their own wood. New machines were developed to make specific types of paper or cardboard. Photo paper (used for photographs) and waxed paper (used for food) were just two of the many new types of paper being produced.

In the 1900s, people became worried about how mills affected the **environment**. Water squeezed from the pulp and papermaking chemicals **polluted** rivers and soil. Smoke poured out of chimneys, polluting the air. Cutting down trees destroyed forests.

As a result, laws were passed to reduce pollution. Mills installed filters to reduce air and water pollution. Paper companies replanted forests, and people started **recycling**. Papermaking became more environmentally friendly.

▼ Today's paper mills produce paper by the ton.

How Paper Is Made

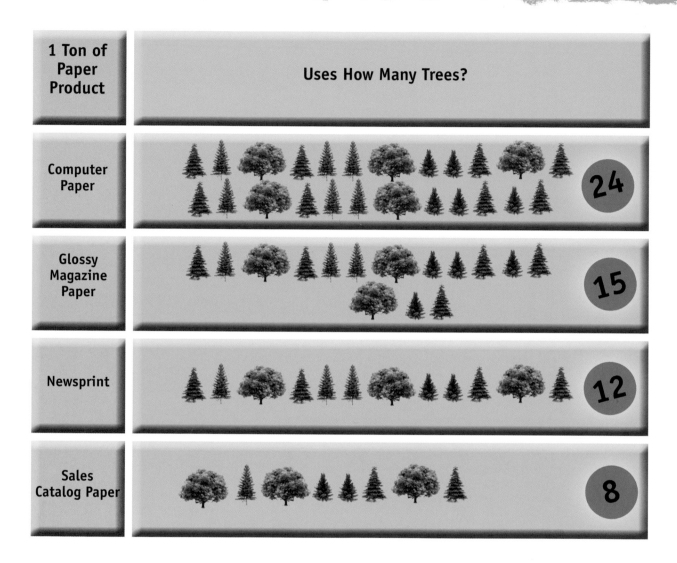

1 Ton of Paper Product	Uses How Many Trees?	
Computer Paper		24
Glossy Magazine Paper		15
Newsprint		12
Sales Catalog Paper		8

▲ The type of paper determines the number of trees used to make that paper.

As we have seen, paper can be made from wood pulp. Wood is made of **cellulose**, the fiber that supports the internal structure of plants. **Hardwood** (maple and oak) pulp has short fibers and makes good writing paper. **Softwood** (pine and spruce) pulp has long fibers and makes stronger, rougher paper. Paper can also be made from cotton, linen, flax, silk, and different plant materials. Even grain stalks, such as wheat, make excellent paper pulp.

Harvesting wood

Today, most papermaking trees are farmed. When trees are harvested, new trees are planted in their place. Softwood trees grow relatively quickly. It takes about 15 years to grow a pine tree big enough to use for papermaking.

The basic recipe for paper is wood, water, and energy. The same ingredients make paper bags, soft facial tissues, children's coloring books, or glossy sports magazines.

Most countries have their own paper mills, but the United States is the world's largest paper producer. Japan, China, and Canada are also major paper producers. These countries all have vast forests for raw materials. Most paper mills use anywhere from 20 percent to 100 percent recycled paper to make pulp.

▼ Through a microscope you can see wood and other plant fibers in paper.

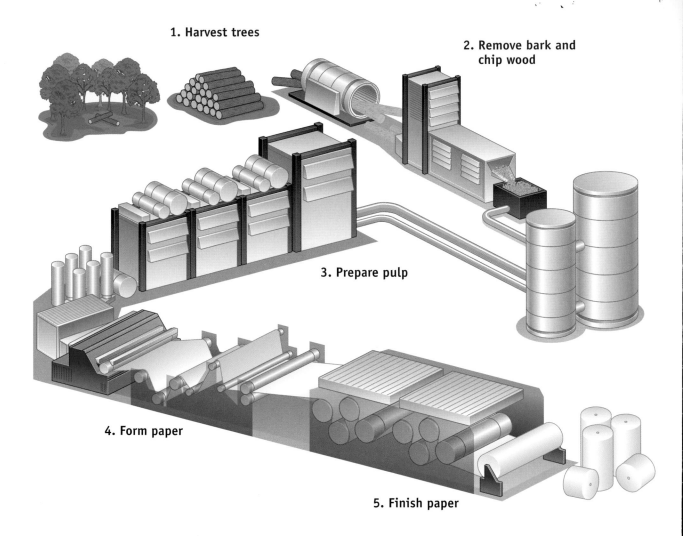

1. Harvest trees

2. Remove bark and chip wood

3. Prepare pulp

4. Form paper

5. Finish paper

▲ Papermaking machines turn timber to pulp to paper.

The paper process

Mills process logs by removing their bark. The wood is cleaned and run through a machine called a chipper. The chips are then ground down into wood pulp. Grinding separates the wood fibers. Water, other fibers, dyes for color, and other chemicals are added and mixed into a mush.

Pulp made completely from trees is called **virgin wood pulp**. Pulp can also be made using part virgin wood pulp and part recycled paper. When the pulp mush is ready to be turned into paper, it contains about 99 percent water.

From pulp to paper

To turn watery pulp into paper requires getting rid of the water. The wet mush is sprayed over fine screens, called wires. Rollers press the liquid mush flat, squeezing out the water. The rollers make sure the paper is smooth and of an even thickness. Then, the paper runs through a series of heated screens to dry it completely.

Wastewater is drained and recycled. Bits of fiber and chemicals are removed from the water. They are later burned to help power the paper mill. Cleaned water is used to make new pulp.

Finished paper

Finished paper is wound into large rolls that usually measure 9 meters (30 feet) long. A sharp cutter, called a slitter, cuts the rolls into shorter rolls. The rolls weigh more than 1.1 tons and are moved with a forklift.

▼ Dyes to make colored paper are added to the pulp.

15

Features of Paper

SOURCE: GILLIAN HOLLOWAY, PHD

▲ Glossy magazine paper is ideal for printing pictures.

Different types of paper do different jobs. Some paper needs to be smooth, such as paper used for printing. Some paper is used up once, such as facial tissue or toilet paper. Acid-free paper is made to last at least 100 years. It is used to preserve works of art or historical documents.

Coated and uncoated

Coated paper has a fine layer of clay on the surface. Printers use glossy, coated paper for magazines and schoolbooks. The printing is clear because the paper holds the ink on the paper's surface. Photo paper is also coated paper.

Uncoated paper absorbs ink well and makes good, cheap newsprint. The paper absorbs water or other liquids, so it is used for paper towels, diapers, and napkins.

Understanding paper weight

In the United States, the paper industry classifies paper by weight. This weight, given in pounds, refers to how much 500 sheets of paper weigh when cut to a standard size. For example, computer printer paper is usually called 24-pound bond paper. Bond is a type or grade of paper. Five hundred sheets of that paper, cut to a standard 43 by 56 centimeters (17 by 22 inches) size, weigh 24 pounds (11 kilograms).

Watermark

A watermark is a faint mark placed on paper to prevent counterfeiting, or making false copies. The mark is usually only seen when the paper is held at an angle. It is called a watermark because it is made while the paper pulp is still wet. Expensive writing papers and checks might have watermarks. The first watermarks— crosses and circles— were used in 1282 in Italy to show that a document was official.

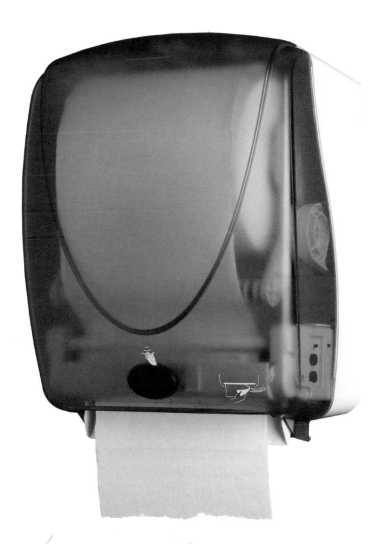

◀ Uncoated paper, such as paper towel, absorbs water quickly.

► Cardboard boxes are strong, to protect the materials inside.

Strength

For wrapping packages, paper needs to be strong. Kraft paper gets its name from the German word "kräftig," meaning "strength." **Kraft paper** can be brown or bleached white, plain or waxed, or coated with plastic. Butchers use Kraft paper for wrapping meat, and Kraft paper is often used to make shopping bags. Plastic-coated Kraft paper protects lumber and is used in construction and painting.

Cardboard can be thick sheets of paper, or it can be **corrugated**, meaning it has grooves. Regular cardboard is used to make boxes for packaging and book covers. Corrugated cardboard is made from two sheets of card, with a layer of grooved card in between. The grooves, called flutes, add strength. Corrugated cardboard makes strong boxes, ranging in size from folding mailer boxes to refrigerator cases.

Paper Arts

Paper has many practical uses, but it can also be art. An artist adds flower petals and tiny leaves to pulp to make a unique sheet of paper. Nimble fingers fold a single sheet of green paper into a frog. An actor wears a **papier-mâché** mask in a Greek play.

Papermaking is easy. When making handmade paper, artists recycle waste paper and fabrics to make pulp. Any material can be used—from blue jeans to old towels. Artists add dyes, flowers, leaves, and other fibers to add interest to their paper. If you want to try making paper, most craft stores sell papermaking kits.

▲ **An artist collects just enough pulp in the frame to make a sheet of paper.**

▲ **Animals are a favorite subject for origami artists.**

Origami

The key to **origami**, the Japanese art of folding paper, is making a figure using one piece of uncut paper. When paper first arrived in Japan, it was too expensive for everyday use. The Japanese originally made origami figures only for religious events. But from the 1600s to the 1800s, paper became common, and origami grew into a popular hobby. Today, origami pattern books offer instructions so that anyone can fold a crane, swan, or flower. Skilled origami artists create remarkably complex figures based on math puzzles.

Papier-mâché

"Papier-mâché" is French for "chewed paper." But the art began in China as early as the Han dynasty (202 BCE–220 CE). It involves making items using bits of paper and glue. Once dried and covered in a clear coating called lacquer, papier-mâché is hard and long wearing. Typical papier-mâché pieces include puppets, masks, fancy boxes, vases, and furniture.

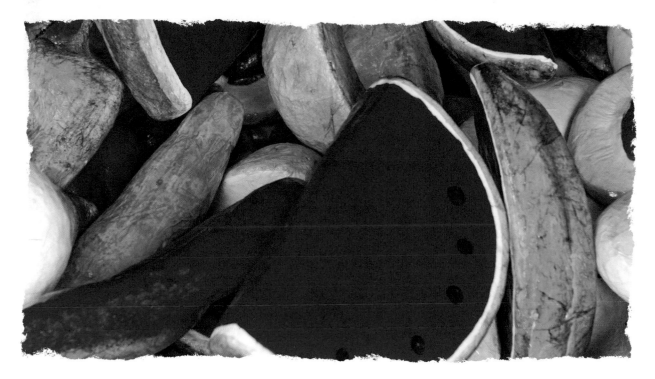

Paper sculpture

Sculpting paper is not like carving wood or stone. In those arts, material is chipped away. With paper sculpting, paper is added to a base and shaped on a wire frame. The basic tools of paper sculpture are paper, scissors, and glue. One popular use for paper sculpture is making mobiles.

▲ These fruits and vegetables are papier-mâché.

► Victorians gave their sweethearts very fancy Valentine's cards.

Greetings cards

In the 1400s, Germans gave greeting cards to offer New Year's greetings. From then on, people began giving cards for Valentine's Day, Easter, Christmas, and birthdays. Victorian-era (1837–1901) greeting cards were very fancy, often with several layers of illustrated paper or moving paper parts.

Cut-paper art

Several cultures have turned cutting paper into art. The simplest cut-paper art is making snowflakes, which many children do. Slightly more difficult is making **silhouettes**, which were popular in Victorian times. A model sits between a light and a piece of paper. An artist traces the model's shadow and copies it onto black paper. The cut black paper forms a silhouette.

Only a skilled artist can create Japanese *kirie* or German *scherenschnitte*. The basic tools are paper, a design, and a sharp pair of scissors or art knife. The result of this artistry is like finely made lace.

Collage

Collage is the art of gluing paper and other materials against a background to produce a design or picture. The art of collage began in Japan in the 900s, when Japanese **calligraphers** began gluing bits of paper to their written documents. By the 1200s, monks in Europe added gold leaf, gems, and other items to their handwritten work. Colored tissue paper is an ideal material for collage. Artists also use heavier, textured papers, photos, or magazine pictures.

 Soft, colored tissue paper can be used to make a beautiful collage.

Marbelized paper

Marbleized paper has beautiful colored patterns. Make some yourself! Put a thin layer of shaving cream in a baking pan. Add thin lines of food coloring across the shaving cream and swirl a fork through the color. Lay a sheet of white paper on the shaving cream and press gently. Remove the sheet, scrape off the shaving cream, and lay it flat to dry.

Recycling Paper

▲ Bales of recycled paper are ready to be processed into pulp.

Most cities and towns have centers or curbside pickup for recycling paper. Schools and businesses also recycle. Collected paper is wrapped in bundles called **bales** and taken to a paper mill. At the mill, paper is "re-pulped" before being added to the papermaking process. About four out of five paper mills use recycled paper to make new paper.

Recycled paper is either **mill broke** or **post-consumer** waste. Mill broke is waste paper from mills that has never been printed on. Post-consumer waste is paper that has been printed or used. It must be "de-inked" before it can make new paper. Even the best quality paper can only be recycled a few times.

Each time paper is recycled, fibers break down a bit more, until eventually they become too short to make paper. That means that only about 80 percent of recycled paper can be used for paper production. But recycled paper can also be used to make products other than paper.

The end products

The paper used to make paper towels and magazines contains some amount of recycled paper. Coffee filters, egg cartons, and shoe boxes are recycled paper products. Even animal bedding and home **insulation**, a material that traps heat and cold, can be made with recycled paper. Today, if a product has paper in it, some of that paper is recycled.

▼ Recycled newspapers can be used to make new rolls of newsprint.

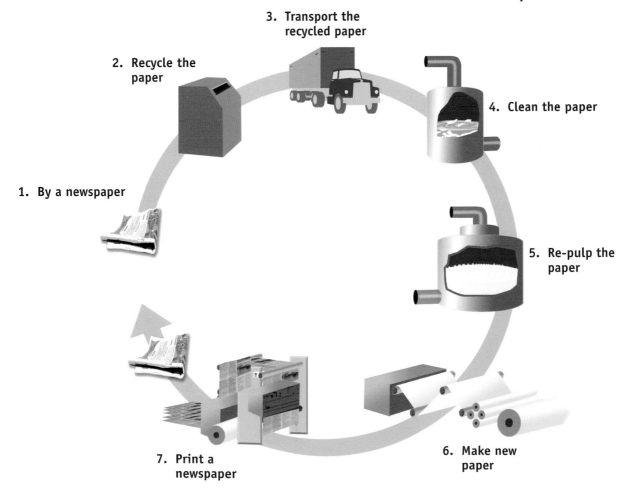

1. By a newspaper
2. Recycle the paper
3. Transport the recycled paper
4. Clean the paper
5. Re-pulp the paper
6. Make new paper
7. Print a newspaper

The Future of Paper

Recycle! Reuse! ✓

Here is a list of things you can do to save paper:

- Use regular plates and glasses instead of paper plates.
- Recycle newspapers, magazines, phone directories, and junk mail.
- Use up the rest of half-used notebooks before buying new ones.
- Print on both sides of computer paper.
- Borrow books from the library instead of buying them.

Nearly one-third of all trash is paper or cardboard. Every 1.1 tons of paper recycled saves 30,000 liters (7,925 gallons) of water and 3,000 to 4,000 **kilowatt** hours of electricity. Using recycled paper to make new paper decreases air pollution by 95 percent. Recycling also creates thousands of jobs—and saves thousands of trees.

The growth of recycling

Using recycled paper in papermaking is growing twice as fast as the use of virgin wood pulp. Paper is recycled more often than glass, aluminum, or plastic. In many countries, recycled paper is the only material used to make new paper.

Tomorrow's paper

Paper mills constantly develop new uses for paper. Scientists have created paper for packaging, paper plates, and paper cups that will rot away quickly in landfills. Intelligent paper packaging lets us see if products are past their sell-by dates by changing color. Waterproof papers make excellent envelopes and also protect buildings from rain. Paper insulation is gaining popularity. And even batteries are being made from paper. The only limit to how we use paper in the future is our own imaginations.

▼ **Biodegradable cups break down in just 45 days.**

100% Biodegradable

Timeline

(These dates are often approximations.)

c. 3000 BCE
Ancient Egyptians, Romans, and Greeks use papyrus as a writing surface.

3000 BCE

105 CE
Chinese court official Ts'ai Lun makes writing paper from rags and other materials pressed together.

200   100

300   400

1100s
Moors introduce papermaking to Spain and Italy.

960
The Chinese begin using paper money.

1100   1000

1221
Holy Roman Emperor Frederick II declares that all official documents written on paper are illegal.

1282
The first watermarks—crosses and circles—are used in Italy to ensure documents are legal.

1390
Ulmann Stomer opens the first paper mill in Germany.

1200   1300

1804
The first book is printed on machine-made paper.

1798
British papermaker J. N. L. Robert develops the first flat-screen papermaking machine

1785
Claude-Louis Berthollet discovers a way to bleach pulp and produce very white paper.

1800

1843
Friedrich Keller develops a machine that grinds wood into pulp.

1870
Robert Gair invents corrugated cardboard for boxes.

1904
The first paper plate is made.

1900

28   This symbol shows where there is a change of scale in the timeline or where a long period of time with no noted events has been left out.

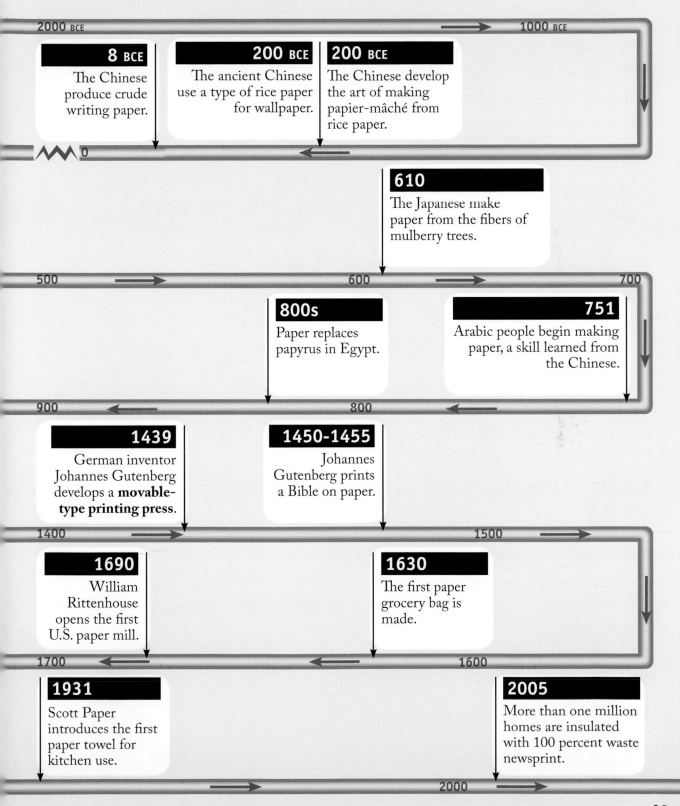

2000 BCE → **1000 BCE**

8 BCE
The Chinese produce crude writing paper.

200 BCE
The ancient Chinese use a type of rice paper for wallpaper.

200 BCE
The Chinese develop the art of making papier-mâché from rice paper.

0

610
The Japanese make paper from the fibers of mulberry trees.

500 → **600** → **700**

800s
Paper replaces papyrus in Egypt.

751
Arabic people begin making paper, a skill learned from the Chinese.

900 ← **800**

1439
German inventor Johannes Gutenberg develops a **movable-type printing press**.

1450-1455
Johannes Gutenberg prints a Bible on paper.

1400 → **1500**

1690
William Rittenhouse opens the first U.S. paper mill.

1630
The first paper grocery bag is made.

1700 ← **1600**

1931
Scott Paper introduces the first paper towel for kitchen use.

2005
More than one million homes are insulated with 100 percent waste newsprint.

2000 →

Glossary

bale large bundle or package

calligrapher person who creates artistic handwritten texts

calligraphy fancy handwriting

cellulose material that makes up wood and the internal structure of plants

collage art made by gluing items to a background

corrugated made with ridges or grooves

environment air, water, minerals, and living things in an area

fiber piece of cloth or other material used in making paper

flax plant that produces fibers

hardwood type of broad-leaved tree that grows dense wood, such as oak or cherry

industry large-scale production

insulation barrier to contain heat or cold

kilowatt measure of electricity use

kirie Japanese cut-paper art form

Kraft paper heavy brown paper

mill plant for processing raw material

mill broke paper mill waste that has never been printed on

mold rigid frame covered with a screen on which pulp is pulled from the vat

monk man living in a religious group

movable type individual letters or characters that can be placed together to print a word or symbol

newsprint thin paper used for newspapers

origami Japanese art of folding paper

papier-mâché craft material made from pulped paper and glue

papyrus reed used to make paper-like sheets

parchment writing material made from the skin of lambs or goats

pollute make the air, water, or soil unclean, usually with waste materials

post-consumer after having been used

press machine used to dry wet paper sheets so they dry flat

printing press machine used to place ink on paper or cloth

process actions for doing something

pulp cooked and beaten plant fibers, ready to be formed into sheets of paper

recycle renew, reuse, or process for another use

scherenschnitte cut-paper art form

shoji gami strong Japanese paper used for doors

silhouette outline of a shape

softwood type of coniferous tree that grows softer, pulpy wood, such as pine or cedar

synthetic made by humans, not nature

vellum writing material made from calfskin

virgin wood pulp pulp made from wood and without any recycled materials

watermark mark, such as a logo, hidden in paper

Find Out More

Books

Barraclough, Sue. *A Paper Bag (How It's Made)*. Milwaukee: Gareth Stevens, 2007.

Blaxland, Wendy. *Paper (How Is It Made?)*. New York: Marshall Cavendish Benchmark, 2008.

Brocker, Susan. *Paper Trail: History of an Everyday Material (Shockwave Science)*. New York: Children's Press, 2008.

de la Bédoyère, Camilla. T*he Science of a Piece of Paper (The Science of Materials)*. Pleasantville, N.Y.: Gareth Stevens, 2009.

Thomson, Ruth. *Paper (Recycling and Reusing)*. Mankato, Minn.: Smart Apple Media, 2007.

Websites

Georgia Tech Robert C. Williams Paper Museum: The History of Paper
http://ipst.gatech.edu/amp/collection/museum_invention_paper.htm
Learn more about the invention of paper at this website.

Pioneer Thinking: How to Make Paper
www.pioneerthinking.com/makingpaper.html
Visit this website to learn how to make paper.

Origami That's Fun and Easy
www.origami-fun.com
Origami is an art everyone can enjoy. Learn how to do it at this website.

Places to Visit

International Paper Museum
Carriage House
8 Evans Road
Brookline, Massachusetts 02445
(617) 232-1636
www.papermakinghistory.org
This museum features an extensive collection of examples of international papermaking, as well as a hand papermaking facility.

Index